Y0-ARF-088

Symbolism: The Sublime Language
Published 2003
ISBN 962-7283-81-9

© FormAsia Books Limited
706 Yu Yuet Lai Building
45 Wyndham Street
Central
Hong Kong
Website: www.formasiabooks.com

Written by Peter Moss
Designed by Format Limited
Paper Sculptures by Wood Wong
Editorial Assistance Jenny Choi
FormAsia Marketing by Eliza Lee

Printed in China by RR Donnelley
Colour separations by Sky Art Graphic Company Limited

Rights reserved: Reproduction permitted on written
permission from FormAsia Books Limited.

Symbolism

THE SUBLIME LANGUAGE

PETER MOSS

FormAsia

No culture is richer in symbolism than China's. In his treatise on The Myths and Legends of China, E.T.C. Werner wrote "The Chinese pantheon has gradually become so multitudinous that there is scarcely a being or thing which is not, or has not been at some time or other, propitiated and worshipped".

From this pantheon developed a diversity of symbols that, in turn, went into the creation of the world's most crowded alphabet, comprising thousands of characters that must be mastered for even the most elementary grasp of China's written language.

Unlike those of conventional alphabets, Chinese characters offer no guide to their audible rendering in spoken form. But the universal acceptance of this script across one of the world's largest and earliest empires meant that Chinese from opposite ends of the sub-continent, who would have no means of understanding each other's speech, and would therefore be unable to communicate through word of mouth, could do so through stroke of pen.

	Oracle Bone	Greater Seal	Lesser Seal	Modern
man (rén)				人
woman (nǚ)				女
ear (ěr)				耳
fish (yú)				魚
sun (rì)				日
moon (yuè)				月
rain (yǔ)				雨
cauldron (dīng)				鼎
well (jǐng)				井
above (shàng)				上
down (xià)				下

As with other written languages, China's developed from simple pictographs, illustrating whatever physical acts, animals and objects the written account was intended to convey. In turn, these pictures led to more abstract ideograms, representing concepts incapable of portrayal in readily recognisable concrete terms. This would be akin to depicting a light bulb, turned on over a person's head, to represent an inspired idea.

Legend has it that the creator of the earliest Chinese script, some six thousand years ago, was Cangjie, who according to one account caused millet to rain from the heavens and the spirits to howl at night, lamenting his discovery of the divine secret of writing.

Shards of tortoise shell dating back as early as the Shang Dynasty (16th to 11th century B.C.) bear traces of some four thousand five hundred different characters belonging to what was already a complex and highly structured language. These were essentially oracular inscriptions, employed by superstitious Shang rulers to seek divine guidance on the weather, on agricultural portents and on the outcome of hunting expeditions.

Of even earlier provenance are a group of ancient tombs discovered in recent years at Yanghe in Luxian County, Shandong Province. Their age is believed to span well over four millennia, which would set them back in the late period of the Dawenkou Culture.

Among the large numbers of relics unearthed from these tombs are pottery wine vessels (called zun), each bearing a character compounded of a stylized portrayal of some physical object. In style and structure, these pictographs resemble the inscriptions on the oracle bones and shells, though they antedate the latter by more than a thousand years.

Whereas Western motives derive largely from Judeo-Christian and Greco-Roman sources, China's are drawn from Confucianism, Taoism and the Chinese adaptation of Buddhism originating from India. At the core of this symbolism lies a long tradition of religious observance, so that symbols are found in richest abundance in the rites and festivities that mark one of the world's most ceremonial calendars.

The portrayal of these symbols led, at one extreme, to the development of elaborate and ingenious handicrafts, embroideries, carvings, paper cuts and furniture embellishments. It also led to remarkable sculptures, temple decorations and other species of ornamentation.

At the other extreme, the love and care that went into very different forms of depiction fostered styles that moved in a totally opposite direction, from ostentation to minimalism, from abundance to sparsity, from flamboyance to understatement.

In this direction lay the evolution of a calligraphy that celebrates the dictum that less is more; a calligraphy that is as much an art form as a means of expression; a calligraphy that serves as so refined a vehicle that, even without any knowledge of the thought expressed, the observer is moved by the sheer elegance of the conveyance.

Of the four basic skills of the Chinese literati, which include Hua (painting), Qin (a stringed musical instrument), and Qi (a strategic board game), the mastery of Shu (calligraphy) is the most refined, and is accounted the best measure of the intellect.

Observing the same disciplines of restraint and suggestion, rather than detailed explanation, is the art of painting, which similarly strives to create the maximum effect through the minimum number of brush strokes.

So closely linked are calligraphy and painting that on many scrolls they are interdependent, the artist resorting to both as he renders a landscape together with the poem it inspires, just as a composer is moved to add lyrics to his song.

In his introduction to an Encyclopedia of Chinese Symbolism and Art Motives, authored by C.A.S. Williams, Kazumitsu W. Kato says "The Chinese, as shown in their art and literature, have an intimacy with nature, with flowers and birds, with sunsets, the wind and the moon.

"To share this understanding and love of nature, Westerners must return to the true life that is a forgotten part of their own heritage, and rid themselves of the artificiality that has somehow separated them from their intuitive nature, as expressed in Chinese symbols and art motives."

The Chinese Zodiac

The animal symbol under which you were born – as designated by the twelve-year cycle of the Chinese Zodiac – is said to be "the animal that hides in your heart". Acknowledge it, understand it, treat it with respect and care, and it will guide you to whatever fortune and success awaits you on life's journey.

The first cycle of the Chinese Zodiac was introduced in 2637 B.C. by Emperor Huang Ti. Its promulgation coincided with the emergence of a unified Chinese writing system and the recognition accorded to philosophy as one of the superior arts.

According to legend, the order of the twelve signs was determined by Buddha. To celebrate the Lunar New Year, Buddha invited all the animals to his kingdom for a meeting, but only twelve showed up.

The first to arrive was the aggressive and talkative rat, who was cunning enough to jump off the nose of the ox in order to achieve that distinction. Behind the serious, enduring, and hard-working ox prowled the honourable tiger, followed by the cautious rabbit.

The outspoken dragon then made an appearance, and hot on his five-toed heels slithered the philosophical snake. The physically hyperactive horse pranced in just ahead of the artistic goat. After them came the spirited monkey and the showy rooster. The last to join the party were the watchful dog and the meticulous but pleasure loving pig. Thus was established the order of the twelve signs.

Buddha bestowed upon each animal a year of its own, which would determine the nature and characteristics of all persons born during that particular animal year.

Fascinating insights into character, emotion and lifestyle can be revealed when employing Chinese astrology as a medium. The roots of this interpretive astrology are deeply grounded in the philosophy of the philosopher Confucius and the *Yi Jing* (I Ching).

From the following guide you can ascertain (according to your birth year) how far this simplified assessment applies to you:

rat

【Traits】 Ambitious, Critical
【Years】 1900, 1912, 1924, 1936, 1948, 1960, 1972, 1984, 1996, 2008, 2020
【Greatest Affinity】 Dragon, Monkey
【Greatest Enmity】 Horse

Clever and quick-witted, the calculating rat can seem
utterly disarming, treating its most loyal friends with
an extra measure of protection and generosity.
Behind that sweet smile, rats are keen and
unapologetic promoters of their own agendas. This
sign is motivated by self interest, which often
includes money. Greed can become a problem if the
rat isn't careful to keep its priorities straight.
Others might perceive rats as quick-tempered
and sharp-tongued, but would be hard put to
describe them as boorish. ○ A valuable lesson
for rats is to learn to consider others above
themselves. If they can develop a
sense of self that leaves room
for fellow creatures in their
life, rats could find
true happiness.

OX 牛

【Traits 】 Precise, Demanding
【Years 】 1901, 1913, 1925, 1937, 1949,
1961, 1973, 1985, 1997, 2009, 2021
【Greatest Affinity 】 Rooster, Snake
【Greatest Enmity 】 Goat

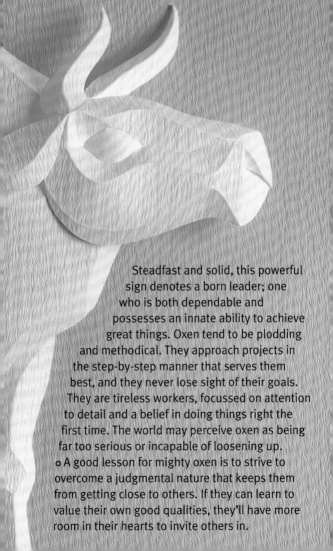

Steadfast and solid, this powerful sign denotes a born leader; one who is both dependable and possesses an innate ability to achieve great things. Oxen tend to be plodding and methodical. They approach projects in the step-by-step manner that serves them best, and they never lose sight of their goals. They are tireless workers, focussed on attention to detail and a belief in doing things right the first time. The world may perceive oxen as being far too serious or incapable of loosening up. ○ A good lesson for mighty oxen is to strive to overcome a judgmental nature that keeps them from getting close to others. If they can learn to value their own good qualities, they'll have more room in their hearts to invite others in.

tiger

【 Traits 】 Brave, Stubborn
【 Years 】 1902, 1914, 1926, 1938, 1950,
1962, 1974, 1986, 1998, 2010, 2022
【 Greatest Affinity 】 Dog, Horse
【 Greatest Enmity 】 Monkey

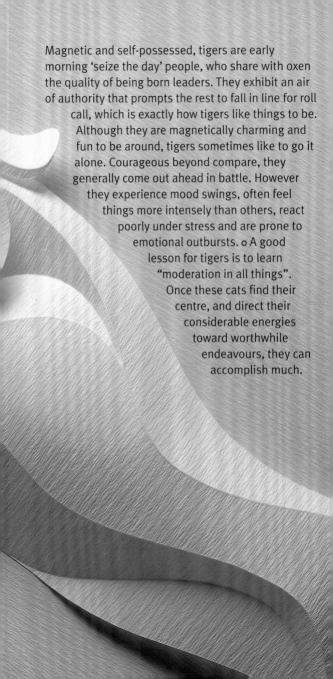

Magnetic and self-possessed, tigers are early morning 'seize the day' people, who share with oxen the quality of being born leaders. They exhibit an air of authority that prompts the rest to fall in line for roll call, which is exactly how tigers like things to be. Although they are magnetically charming and fun to be around, tigers sometimes like to go it alone. Courageous beyond compare, they generally come out ahead in battle. However they experience mood swings, often feel things more intensely than others, react poorly under stress and are prone to emotional outbursts. o A good lesson for tigers is to learn "moderation in all things". Once these cats find their centre, and direct their considerable energies toward worthwhile endeavours, they can accomplish much.

rabbit

【 Traits 】 Sensitive, Devious
【 Years 】 1903, 1915, 1927, 1939, 1951,
1963, 1975, 1987, 1999, 2011, 2023
【 Greatest Affinity 】 Goat, Pig
【 Greatest Enmity 】 Rooster

Timid and attractive, rabbits desire to love and
be loved. Their compassionate nature leads
them to be intensely protective of those they
hold dear. But where romance is concerned,
such sentimentality can lead to hopelessly idealized
relationships. The rabbit is a rather delicate sign, in
need of a solid base in order to thrive. Lacking
close, supportive friends and family, the
rabbit might just break down in tears at
the first sign of conflict. Emotional
upsets can even lead to physical
illness for these poor little
bunnies. ○ What rabbits need
most is a stronger sense of
self-worth and the security
that comes with it. Their
discerning natures,
coupled with hard-won
assertiveness, will help
these happy creatures
go far.

dragon

【 Traits 】 Emotional, Hasty
【 Years 】 1904, 1916, 1928,
1940, 1952, 1964, 1976,
1988, 2000, 2012, 2024
【 Greatest Affinity 】 Rat , Monkey
【 Greatest Enmity 】 Dog

The dragon is the paragon of the Chinese Zodiac, and behaves as if this is a well understood fact. Here we have an intelligent and tenacious sign that knows exactly what it wants and is determined to get it. Dragons possess a certain natural charisma that ensures they will always influence their peers. Sometimes their ego, like their tails, can get in their way and trip them up. But even so, these larger-than-life creatures can rise above it all, with a knack for initiating projects and keeping the troops motivated.

o A valuable life lesson for the clever dragon would be to absorb the principles of flexibility, compassion, and tolerance. Life can prove more than worthwhile for dragons who learn to balance the quest for the holy grail of success with an appreciation for the little things.

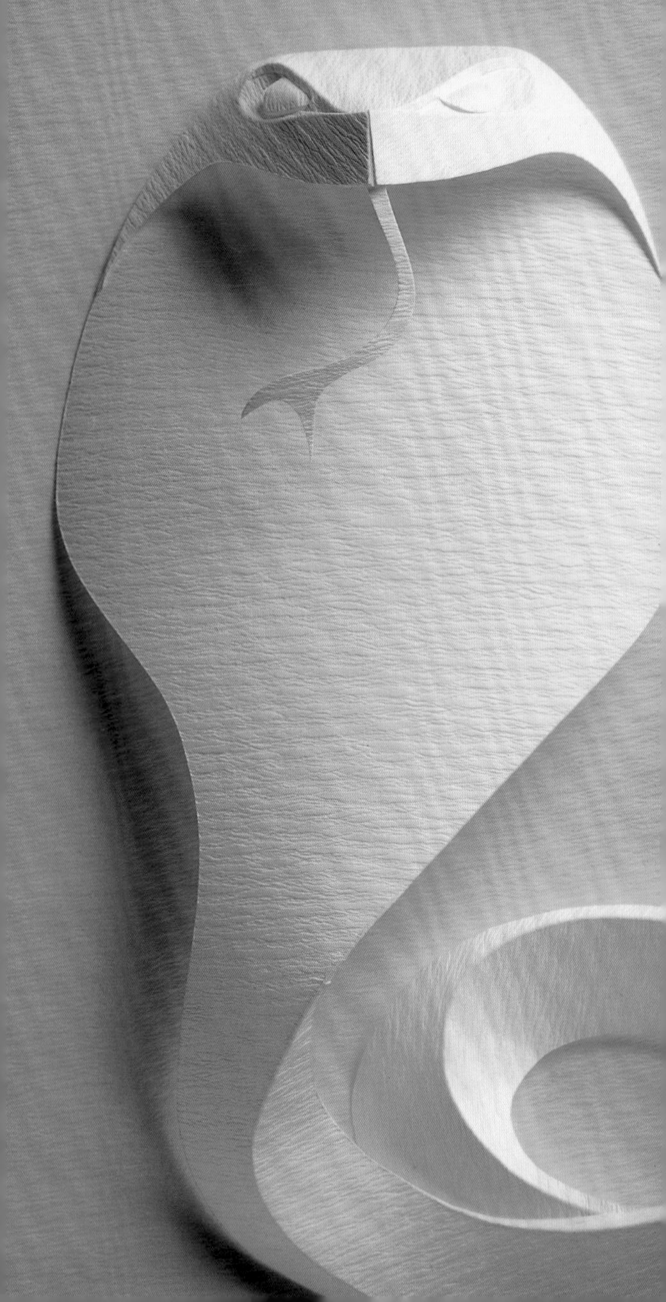

snake

【 Traits 】 Wise, Possessive
【 Years 】 1905, 1917, 1929, 1941, 1953, 1965, 1977, 1989, 2001, 2013, 2025
【 Greatest Affinity 】 Ox, Rooster
【 Greatest Enmity 】 Pig

Snakes are considered lucky with money and possessors of more than enough to live life to the fullest. Sleek, smart and beady eyed, they tend to hang back a bit in order to analyze a situation before slipping into it. Somewhat insecure deep down, they tend to be jealous, possessive lovers, indulging in behaviour that can end up alienating loved ones. Combining elegance with a hint of danger, the snake's philosophical and intuitive mind generally supersedes logic in favour of feelings and instinct.

o Snakes have incredible follow-through. Once they get going, they expect the same from others. Thus, co-workers and employees had best stay alert, lest they anger the snake and suffer its venomous bite.

horse 馬

【Traits】 Outgoing, Selfish
【Years】 1906, 1918, 1930, 1942, 1954,
   1966, 1978, 1990, 2002, 2014, 2026
【Greatest Affinity】 Tiger, Dog
【Greatest Enmity】 Rat

Energetic, good with money and
fond of travel, horses are nomads
of the Chinese Zodiac, roaming
from one place or project to the
next. Paradoxically, they
experience a simultaneous
yearning for independence
and freedom. They crave
love and intimacy, but
often find it a double-
edged sword. An impatient
streak can lead horses to
be less than attentive to
others' needs. Self-reliant,
they can be easily
distracted in a tedious
nine-to-five day job, yet
are willing for the longer
haul, putting in place the
effort to get ahead.

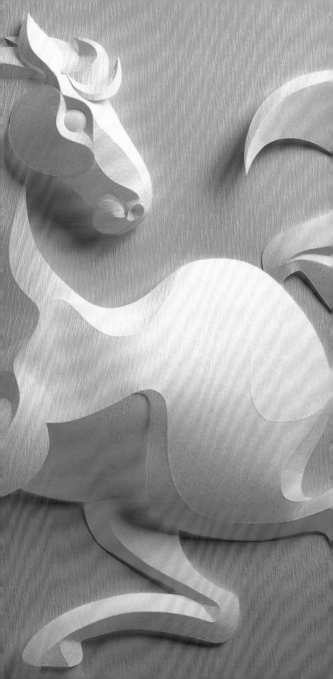

goat

〈 Traits 〉 Adaptable, Unsure
〈 Years 〉 1907, 1919, 1931,
1943, 1955, 1967, 1979,
1991, 2003, 2015, 2027
〈 Greatest Affinity 〉 Rabbit, Pig
〈 Greatest Enmity 〉 Ox

Goats are dreamers, generally most at ease in the siesta of their own minds. This sign makes a great artisan, or perhaps a teacher of New Age studies. Goats tend not to be very well organized, which precludes them from engaging in the dryer business endeavours. Their artistic temperament often leads to a deep sense of uncertainty and self-doubt. The result is that these high-strung creatures need to feel loved and admired lest they start worrying incessantly. If a relationship is marked by conflict, the goat will look for greener pastures. o Goats would be well served by learning to relax and let others run the show from time to time. Once they can be certain that friends and lovers will still be there when goats return from their daydreams, life will be a field of daisies.

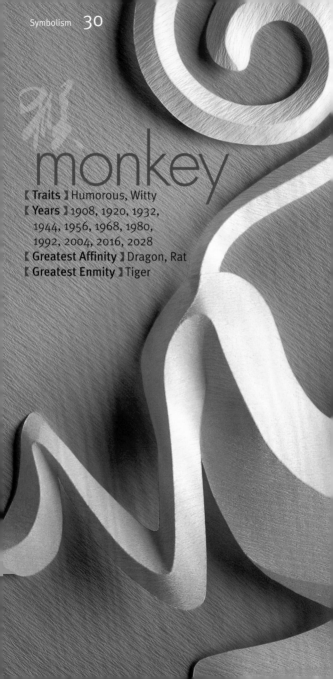

monkey

【 **Traits** 】Humorous, Witty
【 **Years** 】1908, 1920, 1932,
   1944, 1956, 1968, 1980,
   1992, 2004, 2016, 2028
【 **Greatest Affinity** 】Dragon, Rat
【 **Greatest Enmity** 】Tiger

Charming and energetic, monkeys crave fun, activity, and stimulation. They truly know how to have a good time and can often be seen swinging from one group of friends to another. Perhaps surprisingly, monkeys are also good listeners and tackle complicated situations with ease. In love, the monkey makes an entertaining and exciting lover, but one that may have the potential to stray romantically. The monkey's world, full of devil-may-care energy and revelry, isn't to everyone's taste; least of all the tiger's. ○ This sign is afflicted with limited self-control concerning food, alcohol, and other pleasurable activities. While unable to flat-out admit the error of their ways, monkeys will at least pull back and try to tone things down for a while.

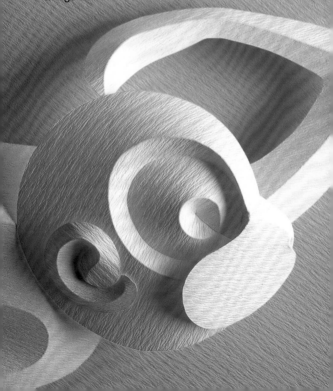

These alert thinkers are practical and resourceful, preferring to stick to what is tried and true rather than taking unnecessary risks. This sign enjoys an attention to detail that renders it dazzlingly skilled at anything requiring close analysis. Roosters make great lawyers, surgeons and accountants. They also tend to be perfectionists who rule the roost. They keep impeccably neat barnyards and expect lovers to share their high standards of dress and decorum. o Roosters' excellent people skills and sharp minds are qualities that others will appreciate as much as their fine wattles.

rooster

【 Traits 】 Confident, Arrogant
【 Years 】 1909, 1921, 1933, 1945, 1957, 1969, 1981, 1993, 2005, 2017, 2029
【 Greatest Affinity 】 Ox, Snake
【 Greatest Enmity 】 Rabbit

dog

〖 Traits 〗 Philosophical, Guarded
〖 Years 〗 1910, 1922, 1934, 1946, 1958, 1970, 1982, 1994, 2006, 2018, 2030
〖 Greatest Affinity 〗 Tiger, Horse
〖 Greatest Enmity 〗 Dragon

Dogs are dependably loyal, faithful and honest. However, they have trouble trusting strangers, and are always on the watch for the untoward. They make wonderfully discreet friends, but can also be rather dogmatic. At such times, hackles rise and the dog's narrow-minded and stubborn side can come to the fore. This sign has trouble staying light, calm and objective when an important issue is at stake. Without trust as a foundation, dogs can be judgmental, not giving a damn what others might think. ○ Where love is concerned, dogs have a tough time finding the right match. They need to work on controlling their irrational worries and would also be well served in relaxing their territorial imperatives and mile-high standards, which can sometimes wind up alienating the ones they love.

pig

【Traits 】 Faithful, Defenceless
【Years 】 1911, 1923, 1935, 1947, 1959, 1971, 1983, 1995, 2007, 2019, 2031
【Greatest Affinity 】 Rabbit, Goat
【Greatest Enmity 】 Snake

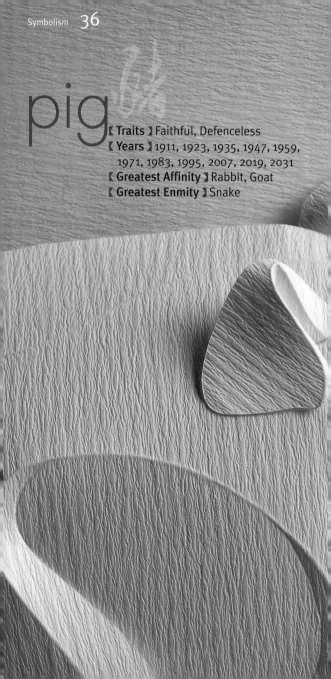

Pigs are nocturnal foragers, rooting for truffles under a full moon. They have so much of the perfectionist in them that others may be inclined to perceive them as snobs, but this is a misconception. Pigs want nothing more than to wallow in luxury; delighting in finery and riches. But they also care a great deal about friends and family, working hard to keep everyone in their life happy. Helping others is a true pleasure for the pig, who feels happiest when everyone else is smiling. Normally trusting to the point of naiveté, pigs can turn quite nasty if crossed by a lover, friend or business partner. Highly intellectual creatures, they are forever studying, ferreting and probing in their quest for greater knowledge.

o Pigs would do well to realize that there's more to life than being needed, or even just admired. When they open up their world to more diverse groups of people, they will truly bloom.

The Ant

The Chinese have much fellow feeling for the ant, admiring its perseverance and untiring industry, its orderly social organisation and its respect for the individual's place within the whole. Chinese entomologists have long described, with admiration and considerable accuracy, the internal arrangements of the chambered ants' nest. But while regarding the ant as the emblem of virtue and patriotism, they acknowledge that it "clings to what smells rank", indicating an obsession with material possessions.

The Apricot

The celebrated author and President of China's Board of Works, Sung Tz-ching (AD 998-1061) penned the following ode to the apricot:

Reaping his due reward, the scholar wends homeward on wearying steed; Spurred by the sight of blossoming apricots, he urges his charger to greater speed.

The edible ovoid kernels of this luscious fruit are compared to the eyes of Chinese beauties, so that the apricot is regarded as symbol of the fair sex.

The Axe

The heavy, keen-bladed Chinese axe began life as a weapon of war, representing vigilance and protection, tinged with a touch of self-righteousness. When not wielded in either defence or aggression, it also stood for justice and authority, the instrument whose judgment, once delivered, could not be rescinded. Emblem of Lü Pan, the God of Carpenters, the axe additionally served as the symbol of go-betweens.

The Bamboo

The endurance and astonishing adaptability of the bamboo – provider of so much that is edible, useful and decorative – have given this resilient and aesthetically favoured plant a special place not only in the art and architecture of the Chinese but in their very psyche. They see it as the allegory of Chinese identity. One of the twenty four examples of classical filial piety was a son weeping in a barren winter grove for an ailing mother who longed for a soup of bamboo shoots. His tears fell like the warm rains of spring, bringing forth tender sprouts of bamboo to reward his affection.

bats

Enduring winter hibernation by swallowing its own breath, the bat is seen by Chinese as the embodiment of longevity. Early herbal manuscripts describe bats, white as silver, surviving thousands of years in remote caverns where they fed on stalactites. The Chinese revere rather than fear bats, seeing them not as familiars of Dracula but as auguries of happiness and prosperity.

Barefoot Doctor

The term "barefoot doctor" is of relatively recent origin, coined during China's Communist revolution to describe a paramedical worker possessing minimal formal training who rendered part-time medical service, primarily in rural areas. Acting as a primary health-care provider at the grass-roots level, the barefoot doctor promoted basic hygiene, preventive health care and family planning, and treated common illnesses. A barefoot doctor is now universally acknowledged as a medical practitioner whose selfless zeal more than compensates for his lack of academic qualification.

The Bear

Of all the bears once found in China, the Giant Panda – virtually exclusive to that country and now the flag bearer of all endangered species – commanded the greatest respect. Symbol of bravery and strength, it was embroidered on the court robes of officials of the sixth grade. Ancestors of this highly distinctive animal existed about three million years ago, in the mid-Miocene Era, when their geographic

range extended throughout southern China.
Now an extremely rare denizen of fast
disappearing bamboo forests, the Panda
might wistfully reflect on the verse of Tang
dynasty poet Bai Juyi, who wrote, in 817 AD:
Here is the home of bamboo;
in spring, the hills and valleys are covered
with bamboo shoots!

The Bee

Just as closely associated with industry and
thrift as is its western cousin, the Chinese
bee is smaller in size. Though normally of
placid disposition, this variant is not lacking
in ferocity should it unaccountably find itself
under someone's bonnet. Apiculture too is
as popular in China as elsewhere, and most
particularly favoured in mountain-secluded
monastic communities. The hives are moved
during summer to wherever flowers are in
most abundant bloom and the bees
therefore likely to be most productively
employed. Bee honey mixed with oil is a
euphemism for false friendship.

The Bell

The sound of a sacred bell is believed to disperse evil spirits; hence its inclusion in the rituals of the Buddhist and Taoist faiths. But in China there is also a historical military tradition of employing bells to signal order in the ranks, so that the bell has come to be associated – from both standpoints – with respect and veneration. When music was performed to commemorate the meritorious actions of warriors and faithful ministers, the bell was struck to signify obedience.

The Book

Literature has always been held in the highest esteem in China, and those who composed the classics were regarded as hardly less than saints. Works such as *The Book of Changes* or *The Great Instructor* were deemed of such intrinsic merit that they were frequently placed under the pillows of sleepers most in need of their teaching. Because the written word was regarded as sacred, this practice had the added benefit of discouraging malevolent spirits. Travellers through uncertain or uncharted terrain need fear no evil if they repeated memorized quotations of the great masters.

The Bridge

Believing all bridges to be protected by a divinity charged with thwarting demons, superstitious Chinese of an earlier age made a practice of crossing three such structures on the 16th day of the first moon, in order to avoid pestilential spirits. The more romantically inclined viewed bridges as links between separate states of existence; hence the frequent allusions to bridges in classic Chinese literature. They saw life's journey ending at the final bridge, across which Nirvana was accessible only to the good and the pure of heart.

The Buttlerfly

The fragile form, ephemeral life and fleetingly incandescent beauty of the butterfly hold a special appeal for Chinese poets and painters. The spiralling courtship of these winged creatures, caught like brilliant petals in a vortex of their own making, is reminder both of their brief summer of happiness and the endurance, beyond their lifespan, of their conjugal felicity. The butterfly therefore figured prominently in the embroideries that embellished a bridal dowery.

conch shell

Revered for the beauty of their appearance, and often
mounted on stands as ornaments, conch shells were
viewed by the Chinese both as the insignia of royalty and
omens of prosperous voyages. Their shape reminded
monks of the voice of Buddha, preaching his doctrine, and
in the sublime symmetry of their whorls were reflected
the spiral curls on Buddha's head, together with some
mysterious affinity with the sun, moving on its daily
course through the heavens.

The Cat

The fact that so common a domesticated animal as the cat is excluded from both the twelve terrestrial branches of the Duodenary Cycle and the twenty eight constellations suggests that it was neither indigenous to China nor abounded there in former times. Defending the transit from communism to capitalism, Deng Xiao Peng, the Father of Reform in China, coined a now famous aphorism when he declared "It does not matter whether a cat is black or white, so long as it catches mice".

Chrysanthemum

The Chrysanthemum is the flower of the tenth month in the Chinese calendar, representing Autumn. It symbolises joviality, a life of ease and retirement from public office. It also predicates nobility, perseverance and enduring friendship, because it can withstand the cold blasts from the north when winter comes. The sheer unbridled ostentation and effulgence of this flower in full bloom have secured for it a special place in the affections of gardeners, artists and poets.

The Cicada

Miscreant village youngsters of China captured male cicadas, tied straws around their abdomens to irritate the thorax and cleared paths with their siren calls through crowded streets. The curious life cycle of this insect, which requires the larva to spend the first four years of life underground, before surfacing for the adult phase, led traditional Chinese to carve jade replicas and place them in the mouths of their deceased before burial, in hopes of subsequent resurrection.

The Citron

Unlike familiar ovoid varieties from the west, the Oriental citron, a lemon-like fruit with a thick, aromatic rind, has the appearance of a hand. Hence it is held to symbolise Buddha's Hand, representing divine providence and protection. The more materially inclined tend to see its emblematic fingers in the act of grasping riches rather than bestowing benevolence. Hence they view it as a harbinger of wealth.

cricket

Two captive crickets placed in a bowl, and provoked with the aid of a straw, would provide the wager-loving Chinese with a popular summer diversion. The fury with which these irritated insects flew at each other caused them to be much admired as tiny models of exemplary courage. Sadly, only one cricket would live to fight another day. Love of crickets led to the evolution of gorgeous paraphernalia for their capture and storage, including exquisite pots, cages, tubes and gourds, which themselves are now much in demand by collectors.

The Crab

In China the crab is traditionally both a symbol of fertility and an autumn delicacy. The Chinese saw it as a creature half of the earth, and half of water, and therefore the sign of the soul dwelling in the physical body but predominantly in an emotional state. Frequently mentioned in literature, this crustacean was rarely painted during the Song and Yuan periods. When it was, by such masters as Wei Jiuding, who reached the peak of his powers around 1350-1370, it was captured with remarkable grace and fidelity.

 # The Crane

Commonly depicted under the boughs of a pine tree, with which it shares a reputation for longevity, the crane is patriarch of the feathered flocks and aerial courser of the deities. It survives to a fabulous age, ceasing to take food after six hundred years and subsisting thenceforth on water. Those in search of immortality attempted to imitate its special breathing technique, which was said to prolong existence far beyond the normal span. Acrobats on stilts performed the *Crane Dance* in imitation of the bird's flight to the Ageless Isles.

The Crow

While acknowledged to be possessed of generally displeasing appearance and vocal powers, the crow is respected by the Chinese as an exemplar of filial piety, rewarding its parents by feeding them in their old age. Should any businessman hear the call of a crow on the very crux of a contract, he will withdraw, accepting the call as an omen of misfortune. Emanating from the south, between 3 and 7 am, the cawing of a crow portends the arrival of gifts. Between 7 and 11 am it predicts wind and rain. Hearing it at other times, from other points of the compass, one is left to essay one's own interpretation.

The Deer

Stag horn is still greatly prized in Chinese pharmacopoeia, as it once was in Europe. Those who can afford to do so consume its pulverized, powdered and jellified ingredients in the hopes of extending their existence, the deer being regarded as another example of an animal that survives to a considerable age. Of all foragers, the deer is believed to be the only one with the ability to root out the fungus of immortality, a trait that has prolonged its lifespan if only because trailing hunters have been more intent on observing where it digs than on obtaining its venison.

fish

Fish are greatly appreciated by the Chinese, both as a staple of their diet and as a pleasingly aesthetic form, copiously celebrated in painting, verse and in the preservation, in ornamental pools, of their more decorative species such as carp and goldfish. The very sound of the word *Yú* accords with the word denoting wealth and abundance, and the regenerative powers of fish – until the invention of modern trawling methods that have so sorely depleted Chinese waters – signified harmony and connubial bliss. Hence a brace of fish made an especially auspicious betrothal gift for a bridal pair.

Door Gods

When the T'ang emperor T'ai Tsung was disturbed one night by the hooting of demons, his two most faithful generals, Ch'in Shu-pao and Yü Ch'íh Ching-tê, volunteered to stand watch at the door. The emperor accepted their offer and slept well, but noted the following morning that his loyal guardians hadn't slept at all. He therefore commissioned a court painter to fashion two life-size pictures of the patriots, facing each other and clad in full armour. These portraits, affixed to the double doors of the royal bed chamber, proved an efficacious deterrent and gave rise to a tradition that survives vigorously throughout China to this day.

The Dragonfly

Emblem of summer, and symbol of instability and weakness, the dragonfly was a popular motif for both poets and painters. Dragonflies balanced tiptoe on twigs were a recurring theme in scrolls depicting the transience of the moment, the idyll poised on the brink of vanishing. The presence of this insect in especially large numbers, just before the advent of a storm, caused it to be known as the typhoon-fly and led to the belief that it was both excited and impregnated by the wind.

The Duck

The superbly plumed Mandarin Duck displays a degree of attachment to its mate which is deemed rare among avian species, and is said to pine away and die if separated from its partner. Hence it is held in great esteem as a symbol of conjugal fidelity. Unhappily for the duck, it is also esteemed for its flavour, so that large numbers of survivors were left to succumb to bereavement in order to advance the culinary arts of China. Ducks in general form a staple of the Chinese diet. Extensively raised on the duck farms of southern China, they end their days dried or salted, flattened and waxed, or diced into savoury chunks for that popular dish known as Peking duck.

The Elephant

The Chinese character denoting the elephant is sometimes interchangeable with the character that identifies a Prime Minister. Along with the tiger, leopard and lion, the elephant is one of the four animals representing power and energy, its particular attributes lying in its strength, sagacity and prudence. Giant stone elephants lined the avenues leading to the tombs of the Ming emperors. Childless women would lodge stones on the backs of these, in hopes of bearing a male infant.

frogs
and toads

The Chinese collectively describe frogs and toads as heavenly chickens, because their spawn was originally believed to have fallen overnight with the dew from the firmament. Especially propitious is the three-legged toad, which lives on the moon and swallows it to cause its eclipse. Emblem of the unattainable, figurines of this mythical creature, with coins in their mouths, are prescribed by *feng shui* geomancers as spurs to ambition.

The Goose

When the Chinese inaugurated their first postal service, they employed the wild goose as its emblem, commemorating the ingenuity of Su Wu who, while held prisoner by the Turkish tribes in the second century B.C., contrived to inform Emperor Han Wu Ti of his whereabouts by attaching a letter to the leg of a wild goose. Brought down in the imperial pleasure gardens, this aerial mail delivery led to Su's release. Civil servants of the third grade wore the wild goose as their badge of office. Believed to mate for life, the goose is seen – in addition to a harbinger of good news – as another of those much prized emblems of marital fidelity.

The Gourd

Emblem of Li T'ieh-Kuai, one of the legendary Eight Immortals, the pendulous, hourglass-shaped and aesthetically satisfying gourd represents necromancy, longevity, science, medicine and magic. With a stoppered hole drilled where its stem used to be, it also served as container for mysterious potions, and hence a charm to ward off evil influence.

The Kingfisher

The kingfisher supplied China with a synonym for gaudy raiment, its polychrome plumage providing the source of a wide range of crafts known as kingfisher ware, for which the feathers were inlaid as appliqué in silver and copper ornaments. Headdresses, combs, brooches and jewel boxes were thus fashioned with alternating azure, ultramarine and sapphire blues greatly appealing to the feminine sex, among whom the bird itself came to be known as a metaphor of all things bright and beautiful.

The Kitchen God

The Kitchen God is indispensable to the traditional Chinese home. Descended from Wu Ti, a devotee of Taoism in the second century B.C., this homely divinity is represented either by a clay or wooden figure or by a painting that shows him looking as serious as his diverse responsibilities would indicate. It is his task to note the virtues and vices of the household, and submit his report to the other gods on the 23rd day of the 12th moon of each year. Fortunately for those who may fare poorly in these reports, he is partial to sticky sweets placed before him as offerings, so that he may ascend to heaven unable to open his lips.

Hawks
and falcons

The Mongol Emperors delighted in falconry, seeing these raptors as the quintessence of boldness and keen vision and source of inspiration for their military strategies. Marco Polo describes Kublai Khan employing seventy thousand attendants on his hawking excursions. In feudal China falcon banners were borne on the chariots of higher chieftains, and live ones carried on their shoulders as symbols of authority.

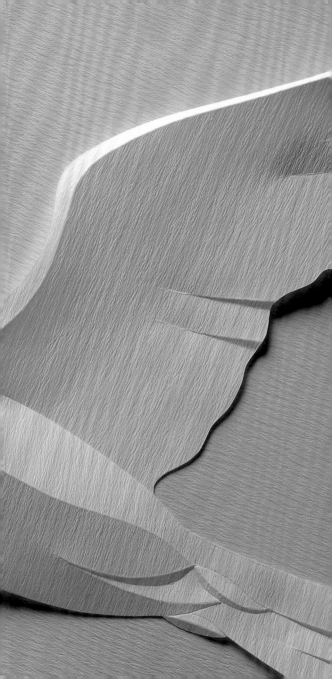

Kwan Yin

Born of the sacred lotus and adopted into Buddhism as a Bodhisattva, Kwan Yin is the most frequently entreated divinity of the Chinese pantheon. Invariably depicted in flowing white robes, she is often seen with a white hood draped over her head. Sometimes portrayed bearing a child in one arm, she is the recipient of special devotions by childless couples longing for offspring. Her very name defines her as "she who answers prayers", and her reputation for boundless compassion forged an early link with the Virgin Mary of Christianity and the Indian god Avalokita or Avalokitesvara, the Tantric Buddhist Lord of Mercy, whose tears gave birth to the goddess Tara.

The Lion

Nothing could be more remote from the Western concept of the *King of the Jungle* than the so-called Chinese lion. Never indigenous to China, the lion arrived – in attenuated translation – as a familiar of Buddha, flanking the gates as protector of sacred buildings. While intended to scare off demons, it has the opposite effect on children, who delight in watching two men dancing to the beat of a drum under a lion costume topped by a prodigious *papier-mâché* mask. Brought to life when its eyes are dotted with brush strokes, the lion is the much loved celebrant of festive events, rewarded for its gyrations by a suspended lettuce concealing a red packet of lucky money.

Lü Dong-bing

The patron saint of barbers, Lü Dong-bing of the Tang Dynasty is numbered among the Eight Immortals and accredited with extraordinary accomplishments. Instead of paying for wine consumed at an inn, he painted two dancing cranes on its wall. These were so lifelike that the inn received a rush of visitors until the artist settled his account and the cranes flew away. On other occasions he turned well water into wine and caused a drinking companion to relive his entire life in a dream.

The Lute

The lute or *Ch'in* symbolizes marital bliss and suppression of lust. But the music of this instrument was not to everyone's taste. The Chinese author Ding Ling believed "Happiness is to take up the struggle in the midst of the raging storm, and not to pluck the lute in the moonlight or recite poetry among the blossoms."

lotus

When Buddha attained enlightenment under the Bodhi tree, he envisaged his fellow beings as lotus stems, some mired in mud, others just surfacing above the lake and a few beginning to flower. Hence the preeminence of the lotus above all other blossoms in Chinese scriptures. Symbol of purity and perfection, because it emerges from mire but is not defiled, the lotus is a parable of Buddha, born into the world but living above it, flowering when its seed is ripe, just as the preachings of Buddha convey his profound truths.

The Moon

One of the *Twelve Symbols of Sovereignty* (or imperial authority), the moon represents heaven, opposing the sun's active principle (*Yang*) with the passive principle (*Yin*). Artists, and carvers of precious stones, frequently portrayed the moon as a light blue or green disc, on which they depicted the legendary hare, the animal that early observers of the moon's surface claimed they could glimpse there, industriously pounding the elixir of immortality.

 # The Mountain

To the Chinese, mountains were invariably shrouded in mist and intrinsically mystical, the high places where one came closest to the gods. They served as pedestals for perilously perched pagodas and places of worship, rewarding with spiritual solace all who arduously attained them. They also acted as barriers against outer barbarians and subordinate tribes of questionable loyalty.

The Onion

The onion serves as a symbol for cleverness, and the variety known as stag onion is worn around the waist by a pregnant woman in hopes of bearing a gifted son. Nevertheless there is some contradiction in this belief, for while women who harvest onions on the 15th day of the first month can be assured of obtaining excellent spouses, onions placed under the bridal bed will prevent the defloration of the bride. The fingers of a woman are compared to green onions, and self-respecting Chinese vegetarians will not have them on the menu.

The Orange

The popularity of the orange on the Chinese bill of fare has as much to do with its auspicious significance as with its taste and nutritional value. No New Year celebrations are complete without the presence of an orange bush, bestowing abundant happiness and prosperity. Many varieties of this fruit are cultivated in different parts of China, including the mandarin, the cinnabar, and the pomelo. The orange, in any of these manifestations, played an important role in traditional imperial sacrifices to heaven, and copious tributes of oranges were dispatched to the palace in Beijing for that purpose.

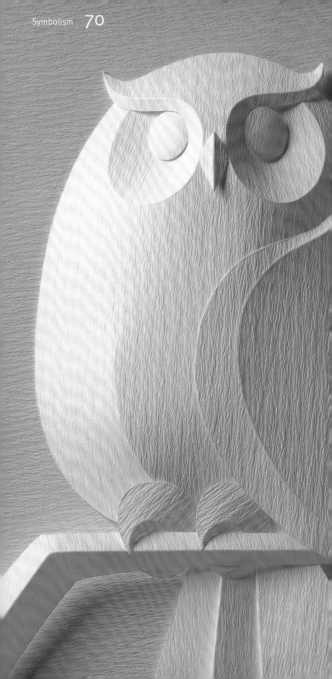

owl

The hoot of the owl is heard with dread by the Chinese, as a call for the souls of the dying. Universally feared as the harbinger of death in the neighbourhood, it is a voice described by some as a cry to fellow demons and by others as the sound of a spade preparing a grave. So ill is its repute that the young of this nocturnal predator are said to devour their mother, making maternal endeavours a risky venture for foragers returning to the nest with empty beaks.

Palm Leaf

In the inventory of China's Hundred Antiques, or Hundred Treasures, the palm leaf is the badge of the self educated. A palm leaf fan constantly attended Chung-Li Ch'üan, of the Eight Immortals, who never uttered a sound from the day of his birth until he was seven days old, at which point, to the great astonishment of all assembled, he sprang erect and exclaimed: "My feet have wandered in the purple palace of the *hsien*. My name is recorded in the capital of the Jade Emperor."

The Pavilion

The Chinese pavilion is the resort of writers and artists in search of inspiration, and of intellectuals seeking the stimulant of discourse among friends, while drinking in the view. Hospitable Chinese villagers construct pavilions so that passing strangers may shelter from showers and admire their surroundings. But the more enterprising seek to locate these constructions at vertiginous heights, overhanging chasms and gorges that take one's breath away both in getting there and in contemplating the spectacle unveiled. Hence the curvaceously pointed roof is more than the mere motif for romantic assignation; it is the lightning rod to draw ambrosia from the heavens.

Peach

Just as the fruit of the peach tree symbolises longevity, so its blossom – emblem of the second month of the Chinese calendar – is reputed to hold the secret of immortality and to guard against the injurious elements that contribute to the process of ageing and decay. Often, in both Chinese and Japanese art, the peach is depicted in the grasp of an old man whose contented smile hints at his discovery of that secret.

The Peacock

Native to India and South East Asia, the peacock was an early importation into China, much admired for its finery, which went into the fashioning of fans and other items of adornment. An old Chinese legend tells of the daughter of a mighty military commander who painted a peacock on an ornamental screen and promised to marry the first suitor who struck the bird twice with arrows – while running. A fleet-footed, steady-aiming Tang emperor put out both the peacock's eyes and won himself a bride. Hence "selection by hitting the bird screen" entered the Chinese language as a euphemism for finding a husband.

praying
mantis

Observing a praying mantis pouncing on a cicada,
the T'ang dynasty poet Lo Hung-sien reflected on
man's nature, which in turn he compared to a
snake attempting to swallow an elephant.
Certainly the misleadingly meditative aspect of
the mantis, with its arms apparently folded in
prayer, did not mislead the Chinese, who
regarded it as a foolish example of both
greed and pertinacity, its eyes so much
bigger than its stomach that it would
even interrupt its contemplation to
reach for an approaching oxcart.

The Peipa

He who plays the peipa calls the tune in a Chinese orchestra. The music of this elegant, four-stringed, pear-shaped instrument, dating back to the second century B.C., has been cherished by untold generations of Chinese and is now achieving popularity with Western listeners. The peipa's short, bent neck has thirty frets which extend onto the soundboard, offering a wide range of 3.5 octaves. Playing technique is characterised by spectacular finger dexterity and virtuosi programmatic effects. Rolls, slaps, pizzicato, harmonics and noises are often combined into extensive tone poems, vividly describing famous battles or other exciting scenes. The instrument is also capable of more lyrical effects in pieces inspired by poetry, landscapes and historical themes.

The Peony

Of the flowers associated with each of the four seasons, the peony takes precedence, as herald of the spring. It is followed by the lotus of summer, the chrysanthemum of autumn and the wild plum of winter. A considerable body of literature dwells on the cultivation of the peony, more successfully achieved in northern China than in the south. Regarded as the emblem of riches and honour, it is also linked with love, affection and feminine beauty. Medicinal extracts derived from its root are prescribed for congestions and blood disorders.

The Persimmon

The persimmon is favoured for cultivation in temple gardens because of its four virtues: it enjoys a long life, provides shade, birds nest in it and it harbours no vermin. Along with the tangerine, it is a suitable gift for presentation to those launching new enterprises, accompanied by the wish "May good fortune attend you in all your endeavours". Indeed its very name in Chinese resembles the word *shi*, denoting business affairs. This onomatopoeia is taken a step further by the pictorial representation of persimmon cake in the company of a branch of pine and an orange – the whole assemblage denoting auspicious fortune in a hundred undertakings.

The Pheasant

An ode in the Chinese Canon of *Poetry* contains the following lament of a wife for her absent husband:

Away the startled pheasant flies
With lazy flapping of his wings;
Borne was my heart's lord from my eyes –
What pain this separation brings

Remarkable for its long tail feathers – sometimes extending six feet or more – the pheasant supplied much desired adornment for the headdress of stage actors portraying heroic warriors and generals. The bird is depicted on a rock in the sea, gazing into the sun; as symbol of imperial authority.

The Phoenix

The phoenix appears only when reason prevails, which accounts for the extreme rarity of this legendary bird. At other times it dwells in the Vermilion Hills, awaiting the return of peace throughout the land. No two examples of this avian paragon can ever be observed at once. When it flies, it does so attended by a comet train of lesser and smaller birds. It alights only on the *wu t'ung* tree, feeds only on bamboo seeds and endures its thirst for quenching only at the sweetest and purest fountains. It will not peck or injure living insects; nor will it tread on living herbs.

Pomegranate

The Pomegranate blossom is elected to represent the sixth month of the Chinese calendar. Because its fruit ripens to reveal hundreds of tiny seeds, it is also symbolizes a wealth of offspring. This makes it a suitable token for a father to bring to the bedside where his firstborn has just been delivered, so that the recuperating mother can be inspired to further feats of fecundity.

The Quail

Its pugnacious character ensured for the Quail a reputation for fearlessness out of all proportion to its size. Closely related to the partridge, this gallinaceous bird was commonly found in China and valued for its fighting qualities. Early European observers remarked that "the Chinese carry them about in a bag which hangs from the girdle, treat them with great care and blow occasionally upon a reed to arouse their fierceness". Owing to its somewhat bedraggled appearance, the Quail was also regarded as a symbol of poverty courageously borne.

Rice

Along with bamboo, rice is one of the two great providers that have figured prominently throughout the long and tortuous course of Chinese civilization. Aside from the fundamental role of the grain itself in the Chinese diet, the flowers are used as dentifrice, the stalk is recommended for biliousness and its ash is employed in the treatment of wounds and discharges. Rice straw goes into the making of paper, matting, sandals, rope, thatch and fertiliser, and can also serve as cattle fodder. The Emperor Shun, who reigned earlier than 2,000 BC, elevated the humble grain of rice to one of the Twelve Ornaments – "to remind us of the plenty we ought to procure for the people".

Rice Bowl

The rice bowl symbolizes the very core of existence, for it holds the essential staff of life. Without it, one cannot eat. Therefore a broken rice bowl connotes a livelihood destroyed, with its concomitant threat of bankruptcy and starvation. The term "iron rice bowl" has therefore come to signify a system of guaranteed lifetime employment, in which the tenure and level of wages are not related to job performance. In other words a euphemism for the civil service.

The Ring

Lacking either beginning or end, the ring signified eternity. It was also emblematic of authority and – depending on the perfection or otherwise of its manufactured form – could betoken either imperial favour or displeasure. Officers banished to far frontiers for maladministration would await with trepidation the arrival of the ring that signalled completion of their sentence. If it were perfectly formed, it would indicate acceptance of their return to the emperor's graces. If not, they had better contemplate still further removal into outer barbarian wastelands.

The Swallow

China's capital, Beijing, was once known as Peiping, the City of Swallows, because of the large numbers of those birds nesting in its ancient buildings. But the celebrated birds' nest soup so prized by Chinese gourmets derives from the gelatinous nests of the Sea Swallow, perilously obtained through the ascent of towering trellises in the caverns of the Malay Archipelago. The Chinese delight in swallows nesting under their eaves, because their coming is hailed as an omen of approaching success, or prosperous change in their business affairs.

tortoise

To Chinese as well as Hindus, the tortoise represents the universe. The heavens vault its dome-shaped shell and in its belly lies the earth, moving upon the waters of eternity. Because its nature is seen as spiritual, the tortoise lives in tanks in many Buddhist temples, where it is considered meritorious to feed them. The earliest Chinese writing evolved on tortoise shells, shards of which were used for divining the future.

The Swastika

Dating back some 2,500 years to the Mohenjo-Daro culture of the Indus valley, the swastika is one of Asia's oldest symbols, with implications very different from the corrupted emblem of the Nazis. Whereas Indians associated it with good luck, the Chinese viewed it as the sign of immortality. A very early form of the Chinese character *fang*, it signified the four regions of the world and, from AD 700 onwards, came to represent ten thousand (*wan*), or infinity. The latter meaning is implied when the swastika serves as a decorative device in embroidered or printed fabrics.

The Unicorn

The Chinese unicorn has the body of a horse, covered with the scales of a fish, and sports two horns, bent backwards. Accurate descriptions are scarce because the mythical beast last made an appearance just before the death of Confucius. Indeed the sage is said to have owed his very existence to the fact that his pregnant mother trod on the footprint of a unicorn when she went into the hills to worship. Along with the dragon, the phoenix and the tortoise, the unicorn ranks as one of the four great bastions of the Chinese bestiary.

Water

One of the five elements or permutations, water is associated with the north and with the moon, whose dew lingers from the tears it weeps in the dark. Symbolising *yin*, the female principle, water is the opposite of *yang*, the male principle represented by fire, whose domain lies in the south. Water moistens and travels downward while fire blazes and strives upward; meeting to engender the ten thousand things. "Weak overcomes strong; soft overcomes hard", runs a celebrated passage in the *Dao de jing*, acknowledging that just so does woman eventually prevail over man.

The Wheel of the Law

One of the Eight Symbols of Buddha, the Wheel of the Law crushes all delusions and superstitions. Representing Buddha's Person, it is infinitely changing and also known as the Wheel of Life, Wheel of Truth, Holy Wheel, Wheel of a Thousand Spokes and Indestructible Wheel of the Cosmos. For even the most ardent believers it poses an endless enigma. According to an ancient Chinese proverb "It is not the knowing that is difficult, but the doing".

 # The Willow

Colloquial Chinese being rich in ambiguity, references to the willow can imply much more than the season of spring which this elegant arboreal symbol traditionally signifies. One who claims to have 'slept among flowers and reposed beneath willows' may have visited a brothel rather than sought poetic inspiration. Nevertheless maiden aunts diligently collecting their blue willow pattern plates may be reassured to learn that the willow is also seen as the very essence of worthiness. Departing friends and relatives would be presented with willow twigs to safeguard their journeys, and those who failed to wear willow branches for the Qing-ming festival, on the 105th day after the winter solstice, risked reincarnation as yellow dogs.

 # Yin and Yang

Chinese cosmogony is based on dualism, with its parallels in the masculine-feminine principle of the ancient Egyptians and the subdivision of the Hindu god Brahma into male and female elements. The *Yin* and *Yang* are respectively the negative and positive forces of universal life, the latter signifying light, heaven, vigour, maleness and penetration, the former representing the opposite attributes of darkness, the earth (as antithesis of heaven), submission, femininity and absorption. While it may be looked upon as a female liberationist's nightmare of macho totemism, the *yin/yang* circle, like a cross-section of an egg whose white and yolk are strongly differentiated, still plays a key role in the arts of divination and *feng shui*.

Zhang Guo-lao

One of the venerated Eight Immortals of Taoism, Zhang Guo-lao is reputed to have been a recluse who lived in either the seventh or the eighth century. His attribute is a fish drum made of a bamboo tube, together with the two rods to strike it. He travelled on a white mule that, after bearing him incredible distances, would submit to being folded up and placed in his wallet. In the mood to journey on, Zhang Guo-lao had only to add water to the compressed mule to reconstitute it for further use. When asked why he rode backwards, he replied that going forward was moving backward, so he rode the other way around.